between soul & bone

by ioana gheorghiu

between soul & bone

ISBN: 978-0-578-61459-5

Cover design & interior art:
Ioana Gheorghiu
www.onesoulseed.wordpress.com

The two quotes written in ink and encircling the flower of
life drawing on the front cover are as follows:

"Our quest, our Earth walk, is to look within, to know who
we are, to see that we are connected to all things, that there is
no separation, only in the mind." ~ Lakota Seer

"Every person, place, situation, is you reflected back to
yourself. You have the ability within you to create anything.
The physiological reality you experience is a reflection of
what you believe is most possible, it is a complex
holographical mirror." ~ Bashar channeled by Darryl Anka

Psst..check out our collaborative project of typography prints
at www.soulsongs.threadless.com
(co-created with my friend and photographer, Ava
www.avasol.live)

This book is for those who are sitting at a threshold,
wings ready.

The breeze at dawn has secrets to tell you.
Don't go back to sleep.

You must ask for what you really want.
Don't go back to sleep.

People are going back and forth across the doorsill
where the two worlds touch.

The door is round and open.
Don't go back to sleep.

~ Rumi

contents

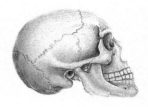

Where the soul meets the bone, this is where I want us to pause.

This is the place I want you to see. It's made of quiet sighs and rosehip tea sipped between brick walls of Sunday cafés. I live here, nestled in the joints of dance, released every now and then by a tectonic pulse. Come in.

This is the place where wars waged against the self left me with trenches too deep to fill with small talk. Where my emotional thunderstorms nurtured a whole field of dazzling flowers. Come, I want you to see them. I had to break a little to let the sun through. Okay, a lot. You know what that's like, don't you?

This is a landscape filled with time-lapsed summers and sidewalk chalk, quilted by fragile heartbeats. Most nights, it's brimming with songs lapping against the foamy shore of a turquoise abyss. And without warning, my inklings burst into glimmering speckles and you'll have to mind the stardust settling on your skin. Stay a while.

Make yourself at home.

And what is home, you ask? Is it a type of belonging... to oneself? To One Self? Perhaps neither a place, a person, nor a thing, home is, at best, a movement. It is when the voice that calls out and the one that responds is one and the same. It is one verse, like a bridge between all wounds, not all of them ours. I've looked for it incessantly. Home. It must've been inside me all along, or me inside it, in this wild terrain between soul and bone.

So come, stranger, lover, teacher, brother, warrior, sister, dreamer, creator —
read with me as our wounds turn to warriors, and our walls turn to windows. You are not alone.

And please, visit me again sometime. The door is always open. And I'm always home.

YOU'LL KNOW WHICH KEY

i was born with these
keys
unfitted, in a field of
unclassified flowers that seeded
every doorway i had to get through
all the thresholds where my laces
tangled, one footstep
stealing from the other
now i'm unknotting the should-have-knots
deciding to let sunsets paint
the backs of my eyelids
with neon sounds
dreams buzzing
door knobs throbbing under ready hands

hello, and the door opens
and the faces are strange
with shoulders like mine, heavy
with hands like mine, pink
with sunsets
i wonder if these walls can hold
my throat
and what comes after the shattering i do
each morning, a little more
OPEN
in the right places
of my neon hips
with the purples of my nocturnal abyss
oh these insomniac dreams

but i have keys to doors
unknocked at
they call that

destiny

hello you
there
at the keyhole of my solitude with eyes
clear and curious
stand back, these doors
tend
to open out
and if difference
is teacher
and sameness is hallway
then we are walking a soulmaze
and i've arrived
at this door, here
where i thought it would look different
by now
or that i
would understand it better
all these years and hallways and doors
just to arrive here
and listen to a voice that sounds familiar
wait
i think it's me
knocking
from the other side.

AWAKENING

6am and the world
isn't calling on me yet.
i open the curtains, let the light
invade me. 6am and i'm still wary
about what i let in.

on tiptoe, i make coffee, tricking
everyone that i'm still dreaming.
even myself.

weaving,
i am
6am
weaving a sun rising in my own chest,
i feel the warmth i was calling for last night.
6am and now it's last night, it's yesterday,
it's the way i wore what my parents gave me, the years it took
to strip down to myself.
here i go, 6am and now i'm everywhere again,
spilled into the world across time,
pulled apart in directions i don't want to go in.

come back to 6am, where the winged creatures
hang their songs on oak trees
for me
for me
for me.
i still want to believe, a little while longer
that i'm not awake because the world is
but that the world's awake because of me.

BECOMING THE REMEDY

on these shelves there are no books
with words that can save
me from drowning, no lifelines here
no anchors no seeds
in soft covers, no tongues
made for wrapping my ankles
to hold me down to my own belonging

i'm going to have to write my own
words that save
do you see them, the seeds in the folds
of my skin, petals of a flower
without a name, without book
without dedication
languageless return, a fire
thigh thick, hip gentle
yes
the way is shown when you stop seeking

i lay asleep
on a bookstore shelf
curled in apostrophes
tired of the fruitless search
welcome, sweet night
make something of me, please
more than woman
more than flesh, than ankles, than weight
make me into a vessel
turn me into a book
with words, like lifelines
lifelines that can save
whoever's walking down this aisle, drowning.

GOOD MORNING, BEAUTIFUL

good morning, beautiful, tell me everything
what does your soul
open towards today,
why is it waking, why now
where is it headed &
what kind of shoes does it require?

we could look for them together
me for yours, you for mine.
i trust those that remind me
where my shoes are at.

i have been looking
for where the morning starts
is it feet to the uninviting ground, sockless,
still free from the awareness of time?
is it hot steam in the oversized mug,
shoulders curling around the warmth of now, just here
just this thing only?
or perhaps it is, ready, shoes on, i know what my soul wants
& the first steps through the door?

7am and i've been awake for hours.
i don't know what it wants.
it seems i've been awake all night,
awake for hundreds of days, lucid & wide eyed
going places that need no shoes.

it seems i've always been in motion,
one threshold or another, some days more faithful than
others,
holding a cup with both hands and melting
into it, seeing to it that my soul liquifies

yes, that's it, that's what it wants
to alchemize
from solid to liquid and back again, through many forms
door after door
without losing itself.

I THINK THIS BELONGS TO YOU

people and the things they bring
to us. they knock on our doors,
doors like closed eyelids turned away
from unfamiliar faces. people,
wanting to peel us open.
i don't want you in here. i don't want
anybody in here but me.
but they come, barge right in,
return our questions back to us.

miss? i think this belongs to you.

i sit down at the coffee shop —
people,
i long to watch them be.

i see you there, and i think i'm starting to know you
i think i'm starting to love you
i think i'm starting to thank you
i think i'm starting to see
that eye
am you.
people, and the faces they bring
to me, so i can love
more and more of my own
humanity.

PIECES

all the pieces that i've been
some of light and some of sin
i'm a puzzle to complete
if i could find where to begin

fragments of my tragedy
fit within life's comedy
and each mask i try to wear
covers only half of me

but behind the smoky screens
i am made of truth and dreams
i am made of right and wrong
and neither one is what it seems

from chaos rises clarity
and hidden in that irony
is that each separate piece contains
the answer to my unity

i'm a mixture of extremes
made of angels and machines
few have seen the whole of me
many love my smithereens

piece by piece we start to see
i am you and you are me,
cause aren't we all but just a blend
of dust and divinity?

LONGING FOR THE UNKNOWN SKIES

longing for the unknown skies
i swim in starlight
and the nights find me shimmering
with magic.
sleep leaves through an open window
and my heartbeat
your heartbeat
all heartbeats
in all worlds
are one;
one thing
seeming like a million —
what a glorious illusion.

i surrender to the very things i can't decipher;
that is my freedom.
i live in the subtle
the simple
the sublime.
the quest has always been for the root,
the truth of all things.

soon
a song will sing me
tune me to the rhythm of my ancient self.
i know darling, i'm lonely
lonely in spaces only music can fill
and i'm running deep, so deep
that the unknown skies
swim within me.

OUTFIT

i wear the road
as sunlight peels
the eyelids of my morning
i wear the road
let signs invade
the logic of my discerning

i wear the road
as if each step
will send the fog to scatter
i wear the road
because i know
that faith brings mind to matter

i wear the road
and lay it down
in ways unprecedented
i wear the road
without directions
but purpose oriented

i wear the road
and walk in peace
with choice and destiny
i wear the road
and question not
the road that walks through me.

IF YOU ARE AN ARTIST

if you are an artist you have been given a gift, a door, a knife
under the ribs
you have been given the insomniac dreams and the
unquenchable thirst of your
heart chambers in flames
and the resulting inarticulate shock
yes, you, with the insoluble dreams cupped in your hands,
searching for a canvas to spill your flesh
acrylic skin chipping at the edges, bursting with each breath

you have been given the overheard conversation, the miles of
music settled in your bones
waiting to be undone, you sing out of solitude and perhaps
into it,
and with tangled limbs of dance you write on the skin of
dew

oh you, with the lust for creation, the fruits of imagination
plucked from silver linings
and carved on silver platters, you have been given a message,
yes, have been
given this and more,
now, get out of your own way.

AND JUST DANCES

in the vast
i lose
what i need to be.

loss upon loss.

i am so empty
that i rise like fog
become cloud
turn to storm
come back into the ocean,
crying.

i always come back to the ocean,
crying.

and it is never of sorrow,
it's something completely
deep
and intangible by language.

i sit
with the body
of water
and talk to the vast
horizon
and remember i'm not the only thing
that has so much to say
and just
dances.

OF THE SEA

i am of the sea. i have always been.

caught between the kiss of earth and water
i am a wanderer of the edge.

i walk my soul to the edge of the world,
hang my silence on the edge of a rock
and let the blues dissolve me.

my feelings cling to the edge of my sleeve,
i let the depths inhabit me.

i am of sand, and salt, and water
and beaches where love walks barefoot
before dawn.

all my life i've crossed between the lines and
conquered one thing:
the need to belong
to one side.

i am of land & tree
centered in my ecstasy.

but more and more,
i am of the turquoise sea

dancing,
wild,
free.

ANCHORED

from the dark earth of my conscience
where my seeds unleash their fire
to the gold hills of my temple
where i simmer with desires
i have questioned all the pieces
i have questioned all my ways
now i see that all these bridges
taught me love in different shades

and i linger under oak trees
and i let the mountains fall
and no matter where my head rests
i'm an anchor for it all

so release me from my duty
of holding down the gates
i'm the compass in the chaos
and a holder of this space

in the end we're just beginning
to let go of taking shape
and allowing life to carve us
and be polished by our mistakes
in the wingspan of these visions
and the anchor of my bare feet
is a message in a bottle
that will speak its truth through me

i'm the seeker and the poet
and the dancer of the skies
and the lover and the sister
of our ancient cosmic ties

but i'm anchored in the red earth
i grow here because i can
because i am what i wanted
and i now want what i am.

THRESHOLD

i've been standing at the threshold
of the confines of my mind
often there's no rhyme or reason
i'm just following the signs
when your wings are clipped by fear
and your cage's been built by doubt
you wake up one day to find
it's been locked from inside out

when you finally take the pen
and have the courage to revive
and rewrite the definitions
of what it means to be alive
you begin to see that nothing
comes to those who hesitate
and perhaps there are good things
that may come to those who wait

but the best things come to those
who, for dreams, will risk it all
who will stretch their wings while knowing
no one's there to break their fall

so i've gotta gain momentum
as i'm passing through that gate
cause my only means of transportation
is a leap of faith

and when i learn how to let go
i'm not turning around
and when i learn how to fly, believe me
i'm never coming down.

knock on every door
stay curious,
brazen,
unmistakably eager

never stop searching
for keys unused
and roads untaken

and above all,
find your walls
and build windows there.

KNOCK KNOCK

i've been meaning to tell you
what it feels like to dream on this side of love —

   i've been reduced to pure joy.

the discarding of things is
an art form too,
as the cement loosens from
around the joints
of my imagination,
i untangle the chords
and let go of the tunes
that don't
resound with my truth.

i release the old echoes
and my landscape blooms
with the stillness of
                 infinity.

when i sleep under birdsongs
i wake up pulling at symbols to
translate my astral pulse
yet no words come close
to the language of sky.

i wish i could tell you
by which road i came
and how long i've been walking,
but all i remember is the

      d a n c e

between birth and song,
the dance between
        now and always,

all i remember is carrying doors
only surrender could open
and wondering which side i belonged to.

SEEK

find whatever holds you without touching you
builds you without owning you
gives you without showing you

find whatever plants you without burying you
heals you without judging you
expands you without pulling you

find whatever loves you without knowing you
finds you without calling you
teaches without telling you

oh find whatever it is
wherever it dwells and through whoever it lives
as long as it opens you without breaking you.

and just let it birth you
without bearing you
as it finally
kills you
without ending you.

GO DEEP

go deep
touch the bones that brought you
into form,
the rainbow arch in your spine,
the vertebrae steps that stretch you into
higher realms.
go deep and anchor your feet there
so you can brace the high winds.
know there is no darkness
that escapes the sun forever,
nor a fear too heavy to be held
by the arms of love.
go deep,
surrender the space between your
open wounds,
let the cracks fill up with gold again.
go deep, release the starlight from your chest,
refill your lungs with twilight breath.
deep
go
into the unknown abyss
to find more of yourself.

listen your way into purpose,
open your gates to the raw.

go
find that kind of love
deep
that kind of love
that lurks in silent caves and feeds only on vibrant depth
that kind of love
that digs into the warm earth for nourishment

the only kind of love
that no matter how far you go
you'll never be outside of it.

WILD & FREE

all beautiful things are wild and free
and belong to nothing.

they surrender not
to confinement and comfort
to strings attached and
labels defined. their presence is boundless.
ethereal wanderers governed only by a search for truth
they vanish ruthlessly into silence
and burst suddenly into light when you're not looking.
unsealed and unbranded, they will remind you of your
rawness.
unleashed directly from source, they'll never stay long
enough
to be tamed.

all beautiful things are wild and free
and belong to nothing,
belong to nothing except perhaps
transcendence itself.
they'll wander in and out of feelings
and worlds without names.
you'll find them dwelling in the chambers
of your heart where nothing else has ever been able to enter.
yes, they will trespass
right into you. you'll never know they were there until they
leave,
for you will wake up one morning and there will be a new
door within you,
a new door where there were only walls.
you will hesitate to open it. but it will open you, eventually.
and one day you will walk through that door and you will
find something.

and it will be nameless.
and it will be beautiful,
beautiful and wild and free.

THE VEIL

this veil they gifted me
when i was but a child
to keep my ankles rooted
protected from the wild

it proved to be a safehold
for standard aspirations
confined my inner being
to social expectations

a veil for my eyesight
when injustice seeks attention
a veil for my insight
for self-misapprehension
a veil for my voice
to garner isolation

a veil for my dreams
to curb imagination
a veil for my manners
for proper validation
a veil for my feelings
protective insulation
a veil for my desires
to save me from temptation

a veil for my wonder
to stifle deviation
a veil for my body
a sinful incarnation

well i no longer want
this veil around my soul

i shed this gifted story
so i can weave my own

yet bless'd be these fabrics
because only from the dark
we have the orientation
to see our hidden spark.

.

WOLFBORN

i honor you
as you howl at the moon

i honor you
as you define your territory
and lay claim to your own sovereignty

this is you
initiating divine ritual,
inhabiting your battle cry
this is you and this is me
and this is all of us
protecting what is sacred
within
and without.

howl, into the dark caves howl
above the noise
despite the winds
atop the staggering valleys
in your landscape of survival
your story is your medicine.

defend your howl, young one
and own your rising —
as you claim your darkness
so can you claim your light.

you are made by love, for love
and love is no frail thing,
it is threatened by nothing
and knows to make ally of its shadow.
don't be afraid of the dark times

and howl at the dark, in the dark, like the dark
invites celestial grace.

let us pay no heed to the love that claims
distortion nor containment
for to tame a wild thing is not an act of love
but a lure of the shadows.

this is your raw
truth seeking, wisdom speaking self
set it free in your primal dance —
honor the war
the wound
the weapon
that has broken you
only to reveal you
to yourself
and
if you happen to meet your tame
kill it.

TO LOVE A WILD THING

we belong to nothing
and yet we are adopted
by everything —
this is us. the wild ones.

gifted with unchained longings, roaming
unpopulated roads deep into our glorious quest,
still looking for a glorious quest.
we are distraught both by stagnant waters
and turbulent currents,
and yet
we were built for both.

this is us, who ask for nothing
but to blink at candlelight shadows
and bury our existential questions
somewhere between the letters
of a forgotten ancient book.
we ask for nothing
but solitude and intimacy
laughter and honest tears
and
that one line from that one song,
just that line,
to soothe us over and over again,
to remind us that it's okay
to want two things at once.

yes, we,
who spiral our bodies at each crossroads,
palms up, eyes closed
and somehow gain ground
and find our way in the direction that needs us most.

because we know
there are two types of stillness out there —
one in which we decay
and the other in which we flourish.
we are the only ones who know the difference.
we change these winds
and let the sails adjust us too.

this is us, who stuff our belongings
into miscellaneous boxes
and still question our labels for everything else.
this is us, who tear at the cage
and fly right back into it
fooling ourselves into comfort and ease and normalcy
just like everyone else.
just for one moment, i want to be like everyone else.

yes this is us, ashamed to admit the depth of our loneliness,
the drag of our isolation,
and the illusion of both.
grounded in our sovereign feet,
we are resilient enough to build bridges between wounds,
not all of them ours,
yet humble enough to ask the universe for help.

we, the warriors of battles we did not start
but sought to end,
we belong to neither gentleness nor force,
and somehow to both.
walking the line between choosing and chosen,
we are the howling souls, hidden from the spotlight
shining in the moonlight
tamed only
by a call to the wild.

JAZZ IS

jazz is the old,
the new, and the intersection
of the two, the pause you take
to look both ways, the leap

of faith, jazz is
the quiet sobs corked in
between sips of wine, the brick walls
you carry, the brick walls
of sunday cafes, all the people

walking to and through
you, their silence filled
with jazz, the old scent of worn
books, the fields you crossed

in them, jazz rises
from the navel of every
great gatsby dream, the longing
of the green light in each

of us, jazz is made
of gold crescendoes reminding us of
every turn we had to miss
to get to the right place.

TRUTH AND DARE

i dare you to sleepwalk into existence
just to spend your footsteps remembering. i dare you to
shatter awake every now and then, letting your
quiet sighs burst into tears so deep that canyons split wide
in your heart. listen.

i dare you to widen your pupils in dark spaces and
absorb the unseen, the unwanted,
the unknown. to watch your ego peel
all the way down
to vulnerable bone. i dare you to stand here like that
and mirror your raw self back
to the world. never mind what they say.

i dare you to unearth the layers and find what you've always
been looking for. to dig your way through who you are
without the drugs or alcohol.
i dare you to need nothing. to allow solitude to fill your
spaces of hunger.
i dare you to be
your own fulfillment.

i dare you to follow your true north
when the crossroads try to drown you. to surface for a breath
of new beginnings
every new dawn you're given. and to love everything
more than you think it deserves to be loved.
i dare you,
said the first breath,
to the body.

ONLY HUMAN

you say "i am only human"
my god, you are what?
and do you know what that means?
but you say it like it's a small thing
like your bones are eggshells
"i'm sorry for the way i break"
no, don't apologize for
the charcoal you turn into
at every abyss of a feeling
go bravely into it, sing your shine into it
and from it, the human that you are
is the beginning of everything

and know that your choices have been churning
diamonds at every bend, don't you know
the trade value of them
in this universe

even when you're not quite sure
that was the right thing, really
it was the perfect thing
you are the womb of new
the never-done-before
the ultimate expedition
into the realm of rising
from a pile of ancestral bones

your feet
have given birth to new prayers
why are you looking up? look down here
peel the temple from your own footprints
find the sacred under there
you are the god of every place you ever stand in

"only human"
as if your possibilities cling to the end
of two DNA strands
as if you don't turn keys
with every word in your throat
and change everything you touch
without hands

as if mountains don't move
when you start believing you are one

your human is powerful
claim it
your human is extraordinary
your human is dauntless and masterful — a visionary
my god, if you could only see
your human
is so much more
than "only".

LIVE BEFORE YOU DIE

cross the line
and be extreme
talk to strangers
break routine

wear your mask
inside out
show your contrast
in the crowd

spread yourself
but not too thin
play the game
but not to win

spill your coffee
leave a stain
take the detour
miss your train

spread your sails
and leave port
stand up tall
and rock that boat

speak the truth
of the unspoken
silence is
not always golden

take that risk
and love too deep
don't examine

every leap

free your senses
and create
use that fear
make mistakes

tried and failed?
brace the weather
fail again
but fail better

push your luck
climb that fence
take up space
and be immense

leave your boundaries
undefined
ask a question
change your mind

push your limit
be a fool
bite off more
than you can chew

leave your house
without a plan
don't finish
what you began

eat dessert
before your lunch

make decisions
on a hunch

stop and stare
investigate
intervene
don't hesitate

swim upstream
and test yourself
learn the rules
to break them well

if there's one thing
you've gotta try
it is to live
before you die

so be the one
among the few
to have your cake
and eat it too.

THE SILENCE AFTER

in the silence after
sunset
you gather your pieces of day
arrange them to fit the darkness,
and question your own uneven ridges.
this all fits somehow, i know it does.

in the silence after
she leaves a room
you realize
she gave you something you can't hold
nor keep
and you can do nothing but
w i d e n
your pupils and let the stars fill you between your lonely.

in the silence after
the movie ends
you scramble for the lines
of your own character,
reinventing the role.

in the ghost canyons
of the silence after
you've found things
you weren't looking for.
that is the silence
with too many doors,
the nucleus of simmering thoughts
and unmet dreams.
keep your treasures close
and your flaws closer,
you will need them.

have you sat beside yourself,
in the silence after,
and let it disassemble your fragments,
turn you to fractals
pound your shadow flat
so you can rise to fullness?
have you?
have you let it remind you
of your own magic,
let it evolve you
resolve you
dissolve the
lines
you marked between each ending and beginning?

the silence after,
oh yes,
that immutable weight
the pause that reminds us
everything continues.

hold your shine
right there, where you are, as you are
the gem in a city of marbles.

don't you know?
it is divine initiation
to be pushed from all edges
by everything unlike yourself.

ALL THOSE WHO WANDER

and i
i have wandered the forests to dance with the sullen
trees in the reddest of my autumns
to touch the bark with my bare hands and
delve my fingers underneath
the damp and earthy vigor
i have always belonged
here

and i
i feel every vertebrae
each
and every
vertebrae in my body
wrenching
extending
upwards
and i
oh i
surrender
to that certain pain
that comes solely with expansion
the stretching of the spirit
my arboreal friend,
teach me how to grow

while i
i have wandered the poppy fields in the
darkest of my nights
to navigate the stars
 the raspy autumn wind
settled on the brims of my shoulders
confessing

that we are but stardust

each morning i
i have nothing
but this:
an anorexic hunger
for wild creation
so elemental
so delicate
and now oh-so-so
deeply
neglected

and we?
we become stiff in fluorescent offices
late evenings, we scuffle
we dredge
and drag
our bodies through the streets
drunk with electronic pollution
the inebriation
toxic
footprints on
the landscape of cement
rising rigidly ruthless
but we
we are civilized
now

replacing compassion with profit
is a modern ritual
of human sacrifice

so i
i have wandered

and listened
to the mother
come back to me, she says
or i
i will take you by force.

THE EVOLUTION OF CAPITALISM

people. places. things.
people, and places, and things
people in places, with things

places, with things and people
places and things, for people
places, for people with things

things, for people in places
things, in place of people
things. not places. nor people.

BRING ME THE ROUGH SANDS

have you walked down pearl street and learned
to be polished and stay still, even when tickled
by the rough tides and the rough times take over and your
laughing
turns to crying and you
have no hand in your shine, well did you ever
have a hand in your shine or in the way your skin peels down
to
vulnerable bone by everything outside yourself
and you structure your spine, upright, the best that you can
dull your glow lest it brightens the room, blinds eyesight,
brings insight
and everyone starts losing layers of everything they're
attached to
so you
stiffen and harden and clear your throat, a roadway for
things said better
if only you loosened the clench
and laughed a little

let the sands through, in and out,
in and don't worry about the out

this polishing will make your lips want to form words of a
different kind
words without roots, words like rocks through a window
(you're welcome — and free)
i feel them hot, taste them rumbling
but i'm afraid they are too much too mad too feral
and not lap dog material

i hum to remember not to forget
this is a shine and it is moving and i tumbling

in the pearless metropolis, hearing things
and this time it's different because
they hear me too
(it takes patience with that traffic in your throat)

and now there is anger knocking on doors, wanting to come
in
(how much damage will it do if i open
how much if i don't)
and windows being broken, wild animals wanting to come
out
(shining is a lot like howling)
and i'm somewhere in-between

aren't you? aren't they? aren't we all? in between
two things at once
close to joy from the depths of sorrow
clarity outlined in the midst of turbulence
and i know freedom by how it pushed the creaking gates
of containment wide open and declared its soul, laughing
and that is the third thing, i suppose

so bring me the rough sands then
for they, too, started as rock
just as a pearl does
and you know, if one decides to shine
another has to polish
(thank you)

and who am i to judge
the one thing between two things
seeming like a third thing
it's all one thing between two things
seeming like a third thing
sand and pearl and stormy sea

and we are arguing about which is which this time around

and meanwhile, god is an oyster
laughing.

SACRED SPACE

define "sacred"
tell me it's prayer
or miracle
or refuge
tell me it's the place where god intervened
where nature nurtured
where the force protected

but then
this makes
everything sacred
when sleep is refuge
and breath a miracle
and intention a prayer,
and each step is a force protected
and each flower a nature nurtured
and we are the gods intervening
in creation.

tell me that sacred is passed down
by lineage
by entitlement
as if sacred is an exclusive privilege
reserved for chosen people
and chosen places
and chosen times.

but sacred is beyond
maps, religion, culture, ancestry, time
sacred is simple, it is this —
consciousness aimed with intent to love,
so go on
and consecrate.

PEACH JAM

it's not peach jam
it's mom's love, jammed
into mason jars, filled
with sweet because that's what
the bitter leads to, if you let it
teach.

it's tree after tree that grew out of neither
desperation nor haste
withholding its love until
the ache burst
into fruit.
i have a lot to learn.

it's storm and blister
ing sun, that lured the bloom
as extreme weather always does
with the dreams of us.

that's how the ripe was enticed
to cling to branches
and fall into hands
my mother's hands
the only hands i know
that can hold the bitter
and still make sweets.

DON'T SETTLE

don't settle for "it will do."
don't settle for
"it's not bad"
and not even for "nothing to complain about."

don't retire your ferocity
for a meager nod
to the ordinary.
it will gnaw at your insides.
it will burst your seams wide open with regret,
send your pulse crawling towards slow death.
don't you ever stop at mere survival,
halting your glory in exchange for fair shelter,
settling for tame sufficiency.

you were not meant for the adequate.

you were born for the wild
nirvana
of "wake me up, i must be dreaming!"
the unreal ecstasy of
"yes, i've been waiting for this!"

go for the "way too good to be true but it is."
you know it,
the howling resonance of
"this is it."
go for that.

dare to vandalize your standard ambitions,
breach the outskirts
of every complacent line in the sand.
seek the unprecedented gasp

that shatters you into a million pieces
so you can see what you're made of.

it will be intimidating
it will be unsettling
but none of it will be more unsettling
than settling for
"well, it's good enough."

TRANSLUCENT ROADS

if we were wise we would know
this is no surprise.
we would know
that what moves around us
is also
stirring within us
that the places
we don't mend
are the spaces
where we bend.

we make amends.

you will see more and more of us blinking
at the world,
eyes like careful shutters
long exposure to the dark days.
we are
shedding our skin in snapshots
peeling our bootprints
off the old roads.

and we will meet at crossroads
raw & tired
faith clinging to the corners of our
backdrop resistance
and
we will know that, here,
it doesn't end
it bends, always, towards the light
and so we turn
and praise the sun.

ALLEGORIES OF OUR CAVES

speak to me of shadows, dance in the terrain
of all we've yet to build here
and all that will remain,
so much i've yet to weather
so little known to plan
sometimes i'm just a feather
that grows roots where you stand

can we uphold these wrinkles
the trenches of our sighs ?
the intermittent voice that stops us
from rushing towards the sky ?
we've worn these masks so proudly
sometimes they trick us both
when our bones start to brittle
we split in different roads

and i don't know what these words mean
i never get to choose
the victories that set ground for the battles i must lose

you speak to me in smoke trails
you speak to me of gold
i'm lucky when my youth evades the secrets that i hold

and music bleeds the surface
to drain my pores of doubt,
i wonder, when the world invades me
if i'm built inside-out

so speak to me in caverns, god
where shadows dance on walls
and take me to the puppets,

the hands that move it all
i'm ready for the fire
creation at its best
and in the pockets of your silence
i'll put my head to rest.
and footstep after footstep
i'll trust the maze i tread
and poem after poem
say all the things unsaid
oh darkness, sweet and tender
i thank you for this shell
for when the sunlight breaks through me,
what story will i tell?

THE FREEDOM I FOUND IN THE BREAKING OF THINGS

it beats and breaks,
reminds me
i'm alive.
it beats and breaks
silences
breaks dreams
and sometimes
it breaks people too.

what does the heart know that i don't?
speaking strange words
about strange people
at strange hours of the night.
i hear my memories bleeding
and i can't
make.
them.
stop.

but i am not
this memory.
this feeling.
this hurt.

i am more
than this roadmap of twisted veins
pulsing for something
and someone.
i am more than this heart
fractured by unrequited love.
i am the force
that grinds the pieces into fine sand

and polishes them into a mirror
where i can look
and meet myself.

i suppose only heartbreak can tell us
who we really are,
for only when you break things,
do you know
what they are really made of.

IN THE LIMINAL SPACE

the way we live our lives is, mostly,
an eloquent dance between living in the moment and dying
to it also.
to find the answer
you must let go of the question.
this is the liminal space, the threshold at which we arrive
hands-filled and ready to loosen.
the bridge of conscious revival
of here to there
of this to .. something i feel inside of me
moving
to the edge
pouring out of womb and into world
and i, amazed, always
at the way my body is moved
to tears, by song, by water
twisted towards the sun, stretched to its thresholds by mystery
after mystery
the edges where i'm torn, where i scar, where i strengthen
the depths deepening inside of me.
the seed dies to the tree
and a thousand times in a thousand ways
i have also died to me.

NO TE RINDAS AHORA

my mountains said
to me
there's more than this
to reach
the gaps i asked to bridge
the purpose left in me // hands curled
around the peaks
and shoulders at my feet
of people before me, the stories
that they leave // feet firm
in human need
to cycle out of greed
i shift identities
unknown to parts of me // i climb
through destiny
with visions unbelieved
that human history
is cosmic ancestry // home
is the mountain peak
the oracle that speaks
of everything that needs
the choices left in me.

SUPERNOVA NIGHTS

in a dark room there will come a spark
a voice, a sign, a movement
a series of words, the mouth of a human
the breath of god
he will know what you need before you do

he will say, tonight is like all nights
when you're at the end of more
than just a candle wick.
a spark is building somewhere in the dim. patience, he says.

let your lonely curl up tight enough
to roll down the edge of your tongue, let out
the word you never really wanted to say lest you become it:
"lonely"
lonely & empty
we all feel it at the same time, together.
we all deny it, at the same time, apart.
i'm not lonely, i'm busy,
i'm filling with this and that and the other thing, with people
i'm filling, i'm feeling... drained, i'm filling and draining
and listening to this song, keeping out the lonely
and sinking more into it. yes,

say it and you set it free.
that goes for everything
i'm hopeless
i'm sad
i'm angry
i'm disappointed
i'm afraid
and still lonely
good

now you can get where you're going
because you claim where you're at.

now i feel like empty space, even science confirms it
slowly, they all left me, even lonely left me
i liked its company in a strange sort of way
but now i am empty, a giant container
a vessel with an echo of — god knows what.

and empty you must be, he says
expansively empty, unimaginably empty, excruciatingly
empty
and dim
because darkness is only the light
catching its breath
so wait a little in the darkness, there will be a spark
there will be a spark, stop looking
stop searching, stop hitting rock against rock
because it matters not what you are doing
it matters what you are being
in this dark room
yes there will be a spark
there will be a spark
and darling,
it will be you.

if love can't enter through an open heart
it will make its way
through an open wound

WHERE THE LIGHT ENTERS

when the aching opens you, it waits
to be filled between the lonely, to be
touched between the gaps
by everything
tender

will you let it
when the aching opens you, let it shatter
the unresolved and long for a breath
of new air, a new life
as you fall gently in love
with everything golden

let it
conquer your lungs, slide down
your collarbones
iridescently away from the shoulders that carried
too much opaque, a final shrug
all the way down each leg
and with each movement, the final goodbye
of the aching through the arches
of your feet, hello new earth
my aching has been waiting
to become your roots
to be the anchor of healing
the ambassador of peace
this is alchemical aching, turning
wound into window, we are
open, open these doors, this house
to everything golden
my world is your world is our world
opened by the aching
and kissed softly in every way

by everything golden

i think we broke open enough times by now, don't you
i think we are so wide, we fit
into each other
because why are we here
if not for each other
for love loving lovingly loved love
can i say it enough times in enough ways
that it becomes the only way

and if my aching is the aching of the world
then so is my healing
so is my loving
i open when i ache and i ache when i open
whoever said vulnerability is power
must've been aching, must've been loving, must've been loved
so much that it ached, and so the whole world
must ache
and become tender and open and vulnerable
like a giant flower, open wide under a golden sun
so big
that there's simply no more space
for aching.

CANYONS

it dawned on me the way grief
excavates,
the way my landscape splits wide open
like sidewalks do for wildflowers,
only more
helpless.
whatever dies, moves equally inside of us
as it does away from us.
it burrows skinward
and skyward
at once.

and i, too raw for loud feelings
of any kind, especially the ones
where caves echo back,
i curl at the mouth of sunrise
left with your leaving.

boulders move inside me.

if i have all the answers
i must be looking for the right questions
somewhere downstream.
we all slowly
become uncried.

if i let your death take anything
let it be the illusion that
i've lost something.
you gave me horizons i don't have names for.
when you left, i held you
while you
held my life.

that's the way these things go.

now i face my wings
just to question why i'm the one that has them
or why my landscape never feels ready enough
or why it has to
or why, in the meantime
your heart
set
like a sun
in my hands.

GARDENS

i know what it's like
to hold so much
and say so little.

child, you have a revolution
starting in your chest.
let it rise.

let the thunder
burst through your veins
it is pain
it is pain
it is pain
but know, darling

gardens only grow in the rain.

THIS, TOO, IS WELCOMED

those supernova shards
which cut across the map of you,
sharp edges begging
to bleed out your brilliant
exalting
wonder.
if you would only let them.

if you would only let them
lick you alive,
chisel into your
uptight comfort,
bend you back into that
freaky
sacred way
you take the deepest breaths for.
if you would only let them
set your longing free.

unhinge your gentleness,
unfasten your wild scars.
let every shard teach you wholeness,
and every cut teach you mending.
more light comes through the broken,
you know this.

patience.
healing within invites healing between.

meanwhile
why don't you
swim in the distance between the broken
why don't you

stretch your spine to the supernova sky
arms open wide
invite the shards.

THE SHIFT

there is some damage here
where the skin sleeps, where the axe hit
in the bones of me. i vow to shake
without shattering.
the warmth
is sanctuary, shh i'm here and you're right
to feel like that.

this is an ice age of heart-speak.

i feel it. you feel it. the need of sunlit hands.
our bloodlines defrost
bringing back an ancestral song,
yes, our roots are showing.
caution, lest we reclaim our ancestry
to start new battles.

we're all native here
if only we could hear
the way the stones speak of earth
and what we've done to her. where the axe hit
where the faith weeps
in her drunken sea. she vows to shake
without shattering.

gather your hands, this is ceremony
for neither victim nor perpetrator
this is prayer for both, as both.
we have played each role.
and when the sleep is over, you'll see
they will not call this wound
nor scar, nor healing
they will call it alchemy.

AS LOVE

love is the calling of the soul
to worship
what's beyond the aching.

where right and wrong
compete and conquer,
love
trickles into neither.

sometimes a feather,
sometimes a flame, it dwells not
solely in the heart.
it's a shame we only look for it there.
it's a shame we look for it at all.

for we have always belonged to love,
with love,
as love.
beautiful, isn't it,
to think that perhaps we've never been in love,
but that love has really always been
in us.

MEETING A WHOLE

everyone wants to be completed
by their other half
they want someone to make them whole.
some are afraid they'll never find it.

but in each search of my other half
i've always found it.
the streets are full of halves
grabbing your attention with their
 halfwitted remarks
and halfhearted attempts of
pretending to have a firm grasp
and a full understanding
of who you are
and which half you should be.
yes, the ones who consider one extra inch
past halfway
as a great sacrifice to be made
those who developed a worldview
of splitting their verdicts in two
the wrong and the right
the black and the white
and have enough love to give you
as long as you're on their side.

they live halfway
short
of being complete
looking to fill
those asymmetric needs of co-dependency
by splitting their integrity
in dichotomies
of who they're trying to please.

so you see,
a half is easy to find
and easy to be.

but love is not a filling of whatever's empty
it's a spilling of whatever's full,
a matter of recognizing the wholeness
of each other
not as a desperate necessity
of two polarities
but as a reflection
a celebration of each other's
already
perfect
symmetry.

FINDING THE GOD PARTICLE

when we are finally standing face to face and flesh to flesh
remind me that i want more than your body,
more than your mind
more than the mass of you
remind me that i want
the infinite sweep of you, the magnetic fields of you,
the mc-squared-of-you.

remind me to accept the solar flares in you,
to endure each molecular intrusion and nuclear fusion that
adds something new
and all the dark matter that i have to get through.

i want more than just your world view —
i want the celestial spheres
of your late night fears and the span of light years you
journeyed through;
the supernova explosions of your bottled emotions
and the expanse of oceans that drowned in you.
not just your point of view, i want the craters you dwelled in,
the starbursts you held in and all of the things you wish
you could undo and redo,
the constellations that layer you, i want those too.

and remind me to give you
the indivisible parts of me beyond my humanity,
find the starlight that resides in me —

more than the carbon and hydrogen,
the phosphorous and nitrogen,
the photos of now and then,
remind me to give you the strange quarks of me
and every uncharted galaxy.

more than my body i want you to see
each atom inside that's made of poetry,
and that way you'll know the real me —

each stunted paragraph, each curvy line and mismatched
rhyme,
the very things i can't include in a biography.

and remind me that we are more than what we are
and what we might be,
when we are standing face to face and flesh to flesh,
remind me that we are not just matter and energy,
we are cosmic typography.

LOVE REVOLUTION

love like the world begins when you begin.

love fiercely, blindly,
two eyes closed, a third one opened
love doesn't look both ways when it crosses the street —
there are no accidents here. only trust.
so love like the crossroad is waiting
like it's life or death or resurrection
love like you're free to choose
and bound by destiny simultaneously.
like it's either-or
this and that
neither of those
and then some.
love like you'll end up in the right place anyway.
love like every wrong thing
turned into the right thing
eventually.

love like fireflies on summer nights,
a small child into the wandering dark,
love the wandering
and the dark
and the small child.
love like the fairytale perfection of fragile dreams
like heartbreak when they told you it's not possible
like bewilderment when you
made it anyway.

love like the electric charge of "never good enough"
and the spontaneous combustion of "you're too much"
love like the fire that fought the fire
and lost

like the phoenix that rose again.
love like celebration.

love IS celebration.

love like the wilderness inside your chest
left its doors unlocked and
someone came in unannounced,
love like it was
god herself
your father
humanity.
love,
it was you
coming home to yourself
because everything is you
coming home to yourself.

love like trying to keep your head above water
only reminds you that even one breath
can feel like bliss.

gratitude for this, here.
this breath is yours to take
yours to take
yours to take.

love like it's too late
too early
too improbable
and keep loving
keep loving
keep loving
until it turns the other way.
love like the odds are always in your favor.

love like the cold brick walls
taught your shadows how to turn to seeds
and your seeds still bear the memory
of ripened fruit.
remember why you're here.
love like the nights you chased and
those that chased you
have only pulled you through the surface towards light.
there is only light.
love like the aching turned to laughing
and the laughing turned to prayer

because love IS the prayer.

so
nevermind the why
the who
the what
just begin
the love revolution.

WE ARE NOT OUR STORIES

some stories write themselves. in between the going and the coming. the dreaming and the dream. and certainly in the waiting. there is so much story in the waiting. the coffee line wait. the traffic light wait. the when-i-have-this-i'll-be-so-happy wait. yes, especially that one.

fine print fills the lines of our skin, waits to be released by touch. read me here, love. read me at the edges i haven't dared to reach. but know, some stories love the darkness. oh yes, they curl up between sips of wine, blinking wildly at the sun. brought to their knees by starlight, bless the humble sorrow that feels real because it's ours alone. those are the stories we really want to tell. those are the stories not even the pretty hands of language can weave tapestries out of. they will be told in other ways.

some stories slide down our temples under the spray of a hot shower, in search of new horizons. whether we surrender them willingly or not, they leave us anyway. maybe it's best that some stories end before we have a chance to read them.

sometimes, you discover stories you didn't know you had. you turn on lights in dusty rooms and the stories scatter and you suddenly forget why you came into the room in the first place. who brought these stories here? where are they hiding? and by god,

who am i without them?

stories need us to survive. we, however, don't need them. we just like to think we do. these backbones of cosmic light, cocoons for transcendence beyond word. we know our stories. we love our stories. we share our stories. but let us learn, slowly and carefully, how to also

leave our stories.

you soothe the windchill
of the winters
i have carried

YES

yes
to the river in your mouth, yes
to the unwritten skin
flooded by signs
of our infinite ways

yes to the silence
pooled between us
to a house made of whispers
sheltering midnight, yes
to the questions the answers the knowing made possible
by blueprints unknown

to the dams we're made of, yes
that hold back and separate but yes
to the opening the entering the flowing
to the camp on the riverbank
as a witness to it all

yes to the wide open field
gleaming in your chest
as wheat-whispers gather, making flame
warming the waiting
of all things starfilled

yes
to all that needs to be seen
glistening next to its shadow
until the night dissolves all need, yes

to the moonless nights
still as a feather
in my wingless sleep

where you
carve waterways into my bones
and i become a waterfall
relinquishing the hold
over the edge

and yes

HUMPBACK WHALE

you found me.
you know me as i am.
between us, there are no boundaries,
only windows cracked open by the songs of your home.

i must've been awakened by your silence,
suspended in the breathless blue,
ravenous for depth.

journey with me
take me to the temple
of your stillness.
gratitude is our prayer
and together we dream the world
into being.

in your gentle eyes i find my first
breath
and my last one.
i am everything i've ever been
and will always be.
earth-born, star-driven, sea-swept,
playing a game
of hide and seek
with source.

where do we go when we are found?
perhaps nowhere
and everywhere
or maybe right here
you and i
and the ocean breathing us.

STILL

i can't help but still
touch the landscapes of you —
the hollows of abandonment
the tendons of neglect. here,
give me of your aching,
and take instead my gentle.
i wonder if i'm still the only one who knows how to do that.

a mixture of extremes, we are
both clamor and still
ness, and somehow
a backdrop to each other's existential spark.
your hands
like a coastline
that cradles the tempest of me.
why can't i help it,
still?

oh love me where
my gentle caved in from a gravity too dense to fight.
you wonder if you're still the only one who knows how to do
that.

inevitably, we collapse again
into one another.
we, the ever-shifting landscapes
our shoulders deep with clavicle alleyways
that channel stagnant water into rebirth.
we. don't. sit. still.

and wherever i go
you are the only landscape
of flesh and bone, of spine and simmer

that turns my wounds into canyons
worth the grandness they are.

and still, i travel
through all of you
in search, in awe
of the best of me.

BEAUTY IS IN THE I

before beautiful
you are resilient
nurturing
wild.

before beautiful
you are dauntless in your elegance
fruitful in your sharing
vibrant in your surrender.

an ecstatic sacred light
dancing to the rhythm of a womb,
beautiful,
before beautiful.

OPEN SPACE

slowly, the noise is peeling from my body
and silence becomes a window
not one but two
curtainless and patient
courteous to the shadows
as they pour out

my shadows have needed
so much from me

between us, all the spaces
where words could live but don't
where flesh could fill but doesn't
where instead, an invitation lingers
and something nameless fills in the blanks

sometimes i fill
sometimes i feel i am made of windows
light pouring in
blinds making stripes dance
in the folds of my morning

between us, there are miles of winds
gathering what must be brought to center
finding rest in restlessness
a gap, wide and humble
between us, a canyon presence, silent
stripped of everything
yet it is not void
for something lives there
in the open space
something nameless, wild, and free
and it needs nothing.

WHALE SONG

we speak in galaxies tonight.
we bury these seeds of light deep
into craters of sky
and volcano ash.

teach me how to blossom
from the unseen.
i have lived so long there.

teach me gentleness
and teach me storm.
weave your ancestry into song
tell me of your longing.
speak to me of the things
that *pull us back* to the sacred.

and whatever it is that you carry,
i promise,
i will carry with you.

DEW ON THE SKIN OF MORNING

if i didn't know what diamonds were, i'd think
they were dew drops left behind on purpose by the
first autumn rain, the purpose being
that when i look at them i glisten
with diamonds in my own eyes;
for what good are diamonds
if we don't recognize them
in ourselves?

if i didn't know where my bed was
i'd wander barefoot towards the waiting ocean
(water always seems like it is waiting)
and slip underneath it, eyes closed in surrender
like i do under the rain
like i do under a waterfall
like i do under the dew drops when i become tiny and
precious
and, dreamfully, i would drag the tide over my sleep
fall and keep falling
deeper, keep sinking
until the dolphins wake me with their play.
i always want to wake up into laughter.

if i didn't know what heaven was
i'd say it was the feeling of dipping your hand into a sack full
of beans
or seeing a double rainbow
or watching a bee on a rock catching its breath, two pollen
sacks filled
and remembering the honey you put in your tea each
morning
and the work it all took
for all the things in your life to reach and fill you

for the beans to be collected, and dried, and packed
brought to the center of town, sold
as the mist tangled with the sunrays and heaven laughed so
hard it
spat a double rainbow.
i'd say heaven is on the other side of it
but a rainbow is a full circle.

i am overflowing.

if i didn't know, but i do know
that all this wind and fire and scorching straw is quenched
eventually,
and that pollen sacks get heavy sometimes
(but we must press on)
i would've become a well, an endless well
poised at the center of town,
filled with dew drops, waiting —

and maybe i did
and you are drinking every word
and if i didn't know
that thirst and dew drop are one and the same
i'd say, you too
are glistening.

SUMMER, TAKE ME WITH YOU

 summer, take me with you.
whenever you decide the
valleys are filled to the brink
with
cricket chirps and purple
blossoms
and you haul your sunshine
into the trunk and drive
down that moonlit road,
take me with you. wake me up from my interstellar sleep,
i'll drive. i'll take us wherever your jasmine lips tell me to go.

we'll take rest stops between the landmarks and chase that
watermelon spunk up the city streets. there will be a theme
song to every sunset.
a falling star for every blessing. each night, the crickets teach
us that gratitude
is the only prayer. wouldn't you say so?
we'll be lost in the right direction, as always, you and i
summer. and oh it will feel so good.
chasing that barefooted laughter into the sun-scorched hills,
looking for untaken roads. no fear of the unknown for us. not
now, not ever. weren't you born for leaps of faith?
and wasn't i?
our thirst has always been quenched by crystal springs
emerging from between the cracks of unstoppable desire and
ultimate trust. and this vessel i carry, day after day, has been
filled with water that i can now give to the thirsty.

i've been ripening with you, summer. i've been sweetened by
an ocean song and kissed in every way by everything golden.
so take me with you when you go. don't leave me hanging
from this orchard, untasted.

like you, i've been yearning to fill spaces and people with everything sweet. you and i are made of wanderlust and wanderdust, rising from the footprints of new visions for the world. times are hard for dreamers, love. but i'll build us a sandcastle where you may keep the seashells that ever sang to your heart.

i've always loved you loving me. the way you nourish. the way your warmth keeps me awake at night, scribling flames into paper. the way i never get too tired to watch the stars ignite your spine. the way the palm trees tremble in your dance. you're beautiful. and i know beautiful things are always wild and free. i know you must go now. hold on to your bliss, summer. i'm coming with you.

harmony is a slow dance, it seems,
a type of giving in to source
while living out through it

LOVE FOUND IN THE WANDERING

lost in the wheat, are you
feeling all directions at once
and love calls, magenta loud
out the corner of a page

answer it —
in words, in gaps and glances, what have you
to give
that whisper a chance to be right

reach so you can be reached
all that is found must be lost first
this is the dance

and it pulls you
beyond the page
beyond story
and all the borders you placed
between you and everything,
moving you
into the unknown field, dancing
lost in the wheat, are you

MY BLOOD WHISPERS SOMETHING

my blood whispers something:
dance,
rise from your skin
dance and nothing more.

i let the universe play me,
love sing me
strip me
shake me restless
and with every note
i find myself plucked from the source.

sometimes i'm a tamed lullaby
trespassing on wild land
guided by nothing more than
an intense pulse.

sometimes i'm a glissando rumbling
like hot lava under an ocean floor
unleashed between the cracks
and humbled by a cooling wave.

dance,
i've been called
by dance
i've been nurtured
and by dance
i've been shattered
like a fragile shell
bursting at the seams to make space
for birth.

DREAM, SEED, SPROUT

holding its shatter curled in the womb,
the seed knows when it's time.
quiet, dark, patient.
storms have passed, watering the ardour, inching the burst.
and it comes.
just like that, an elemental pull
to be more
oh yes, the wildfire spark
the explosive momentum of a thousand suns.

and she breaks.

and she breaks and she opens and she severs the ties
to the safety
of the shell
and it hurts but it gives
so much more than it takes.
shattering always gives so much more than it takes.

after all, sprouting is
the carrying of the aching in one hand and of love in the
other.

quiet, dark, ready — ooh, the earth awaits
her dance
to the depths of nourishment
and she spreads, and she seeks, and she bares her roots
along everything untraveled.

and the earth invites
and the sun extends
and the air fills the lungs that dreamed of breathing
before breath was ever known.

OUT OF BODY

i lost her
in the music.

i lost the woman i inhabit,
peeled myself gently away
from her body.
drum beats settled in her hips
and guitar strums rushed like
thunder through her veins,
pushing me out past the edges
of her rib cage.

and when i
swelled beyond her skin
and into the crowd,
i realized
i am more than her.

like a passing breeze,
i inhabit her body.
i have come to know the earth
through her eyes
felt the bark of trees
only as her fingers tangled with the forest.

i am more than her
yet nothing without her.

now she is dancing there,
laughter settling in her chest,
a body among bodies.
and i want to go back,
back into her home

into the only place where i can feel
music as a fire down a spine.

CHRYSALIS

i came here for the peeling art
of becoming undone
from the cocoon i made
under twisted trees
with my silkworm hands
with my succulent eyes
that know how to hold their water

some seams are made for bursting
some for holding
and i, for asking
which is which;
because love needs humble fingers
when the heart opens,
layers peeling
the raw revealing, sooner or later
people and things tug at you and your butterfly wings
much sooner than later
but, who are we to say

not now, not like that!
leave me with my layers!
to love myself
deeper longer more
&more &more &more
than you give me time for

do you also weep
for your layers?
the comfort leaving,
the edge waiting for your flight —
but the layers, oh the layers i made
with my silkworm hands…

come forth
blink at the world, darling
blink at the world however many times it takes
to see that it's yours, to see that it's for you
and you for it, waiting,

the trees, growing sideways
twisting away from the blade,
the sea too drunk to speak
about the bees
dropping out of the sky
with lead in their eyes —

come forth, butterfly
leave your childhood,
the world needs you
weightless.

SURRENDER IS A TYPE OF ART

mmm and when you fall
when you finally let the sorrow
burst through
the skin of your back,
with the anchor in your ribs, hot
with heartache
your feathers ruffling
in the wild air
oh you will find an edge out there
on the high plains
and there will be nothing
to lose
but your paperweights
let the air find you
wanting
find you
destroyed
bones and aches and limbs and all
to the edge go and fall, darling
fall until your falling
turns to flying

PURPOSE IS A MOVEMENT

and when you learn how to love,
purpose finds you.
because you learn how to give
how to connect
how to relate
how to receive
how to allow
how to heal
how to experience
how to create.
you learn what your heart is for
and where the edges of it go —
how far, how wide, how much can enter
and how deeply it moves you.
and when you learn how to be moved by love
only then
can you start moving the world.
and that is your purpose —
to move the world and simultaneously
be moved by it.

TO LOVE WHERE YOU'RE AT

to love where you're at, even if
clinging to the edge of
upturned wings
even if coiled into the lonely
and the corners refuse to cradle your round
well, at least you know you weren't built for corners
and still, you must love yourself out of them.

i like it when the sky blinks in copper;
there's something about a day ending
that makes every landscape worthy
and ripe.

between sips of tea, there is a space occupied
by the real things we want to say.
let us listen with something besides ears
speak with something besides mouths.
i can never tell when it's okay to step into the nameless.
or out of it.
some people have a presence where truth doesn't feel like
trespassing.

tell me how it's so easy to forget
that the light of the moon
doesn't belong to it.

so what, then, really belongs to us
when love is only experienced
when we give it away?

freedom, then, must be about what we are ready to release.
i always knew freedom and love belong together.

and i say love can always meet you where you're at.
especially in your freedom.
with the baggage, in the wide open leap,
the flight between the old and the new.
love will always be there,
waiting for you to turn your corners
into craters
and your given into gift.

TO BE AN ARTIST

perhaps it is
that in the natural habitat
of self-expression
we forget to heed the warning:
"do not lean over the edge of the world"
and so we trespass

and when two eyes close
a third one opens
it seeks not the destination
the completed
the applause
it thrives only for the movement
the tidal dance of color and word,
bursting through skin
the veins dangerously swollen
with mystery.

these are the dreams from which
we never wake,
our souls dangling there
over the edge
in the hands that hold us
without touching.

TELOS

what have you come to teach me
and in what language do i let you in
shasta, this grace feels beyond me
and my human
my "only human" ness
and the power
and the grandeur you tell me i have yet to claim.

it is error after error
flaw upon flaw
steps taken back, retracing my ways
but wanting & wanting & wanting to learn,
i persist, and insist, and resist.
above all, i dance
like the wheat at the hem of your dress
in forgiveness of all this forgetfulness.

i hear you in purple, ringing the forest awake
startling the water into crispness, hear you chanting and
rising, through the ice a warmth, a humming, deep & ancient
surfaces, pulls me in, deep & sacred
a door, a hundred doors, mouths and ears, a porous
mountain, filling me
i am all ears, curled in the poppy field
asleep in your lap

and you are inside me, deep & ancient, a mountain
rumbling in stories
i am listening now, to everything and everybody
because it is you speaking
in symbols, filling me to the brim
of my wanting to know more, to be more
to become gateway

to become rising mountain
a soulful whisperer
for the ears in my lap

shasta, because of you
i went to sleep all ears
and woke up all mouth
and now i am ready.

DARLING, IT HAS BEEN SUCH A LONG JOURNEY

But you've been made for it, you know. No complacency and stillness for you. No. You were born to move. Long before your feet could walk across borders, your mind leaped boundaries and spread wings over rugged landscapes unknown. You were born for the unmapped.

Never like the rest of them. The bloom where you're planted, the better safe than sorry, the wait for the right moment. No. Not you. The restless was too unyielding. Chronic, incessant, unabated. It tugged at your sheets each morning, started revolutions in your chest. But the restless was your cure, you know.

Without it, you would've been cornered between the too much and the not good enough, gripped by the teeth of false hopes. You would've let the rough times turn into sandpaper years and you would've eventually dissolved into red dust. The restless is what saved you.

Because you were born for the barefoot days, the sunkissed wide-open road. You were made for the caves of moonlight, following your raindance deep into the mountains until a song was born. Earthborn, seaswept, star driven - in your bones there were drumbeats waiting to unfold and you learned how to dance with the storms. Oh yes, these landscapes loved your wild.

Don't you see it, darling? You're gifted with unchained
longings, roaming unpopulated roads deep into your glorious
quest, still looking for a glorious quest. Yes, you, ashamed to
admit the depth of your loneliness, the drag of your
isolation, and the illusion of both. Oh how many ways you've
grown, my dear, by answering the restless.. by traveling
beyond the edges of these man-made maps.

feed the story that heals
come home to the eternal soul
back to the place
you only think you've left

BONEDEEP

up until now, bones is what
you've gathered, to fortify
your ribcage empire
where you keep your
weapon of mass
creation
salvation, or whatever that
ventricular ticker of yours does. you
stacked bone upon bone
for your architecture of ascent, we know,
you're made of skyward vertebrae
dreams.

and now

take your backbone faith, drape
your best flesh over it, let
the wounds make windows of you
and yield your careful anatomy
to the whims of love.
trust me, there is no other way —
you either love
or shatter.

WITH ALL YOUR HEART

what do you mean
ALL
since when
did the world
deserve it all
and what will be left
of me
after
and what if all
is too little
or too much
what if all is
terrifying - loud - appalling
masterfully deviant
shockingly taboo
AND WHY ALL
that i am
is in a chambered organ
the size of my fist
and all that it fits
isn't much
at all
to give away
with these little hands
of mine
will i applaud
for myself
for all
i gave
and where it all went
off without me
into the wormhole
of allness

or took me with
and came back
with more
as i dissolved
became the will
of the cosmos
surrendered
all
the nothing i really had
and was given
more
than i could ever keep

KUNDALINI

spines are something
we carry
in the soft of us, where the humble sleeps where
kindness dreams
glazed by lights
that sparkle and dim
the out and the in of our
rosefilled skins
that reveal our maps
with their treasures
and traps

leave me
unplucked
from the source and
unmapped
from the course of
my spine rising
from the vertebrae deep, a forward momentum
from my lumbar sleep
awake and breathing
our chests will heave
with stories no books can hold nor conceive

upwards and rising
page after page
plots that can barely
carry their own age
i curl and i open
i bend and i twist
a dance between what i allow and resist
i was built for this
you were built for this

a backbone of light when the dark insists
and we carry its weight
the alignment within
this cosmic convergence
inside sapien skin.

EVEN YOU

everything heals.
in one lifetime or another,
the parts arrive at wholeness,
the longing turns to belonging,
loneliness gathers to be heard
by all who feel the folds of timelessness pressing heavy on
their depths.
i have been here a long time, watching.

in pieces and without them,
i've been searching the eyes of whatever looks at me —
and right through.
through is a key. use it. turn it inside yourself.

if there is hurting, there is healing — look through it.
if there is leaving, there is coming — look through it.
whatever's empty will be filled first.
all moves towards harmony.

even you. even this
is a dance
of arrival.

BECOMING SKY

this is me with
the flight in my shoulders
the seed in my spine
poised to meet the other half
of myself.
me, looking for wings, how to be be root and branch at once,
to fill the landscape of words that have become my soul.

the hand on my back
is my own comfort
holding me
back —
forgive me
for the times i want to curl
back
into my own center —
but when i go forth, i don't open
i burst & detonate
i shatter & split
sideways into the spring.

and from the outside, i still look like a gentle thing.
you see, whoever loved me
never started
from the outside in.

my hollows widen and i let them
fill with memories i have yet to make
and i ache
with places i have yet to see
and people i have yet to startle
(in the best of times, we uproot each other)
because we hold ourselves together quite well

until we can't contain, and meadows start growing where we
burst, and hopefully we burst together, all at the same time
open, raw and wide, our eyelids clinging
to the moonlight because hope never leaves the dark skies.
a grand love requires a bigger space and i still fear
looking so immensely empty.

opening burns.
and that is, perhaps, the first thing
a flower says when it first meets the sun.

and we learn how to claim our expansion, how to corner
danger by a wolf howl
let them pull our edges forward. if you have a fear,
that is a door. if you have a scar, or a longing, or a loneliness
so big it almost swallows you whole,
that is a quest, a sun, a seed you will lose to become forest.
but on the way
it is the stretching that hurts. and the opening. and the
welcoming of what ensues.

the other half of myself, i suppose
is whatever meets me where i'm at.
hello, welcome, this is me
with a sun setting at the back of my throat
chocking mid-horizon,
breathing wildfire
into my morning coffee.
pardon the stardust.
will you join?

if i have flight in my shoulders,
you must be wind.

don't you sometimes marvel at

the people and things that have been looking for you
for the home you are
for the rainbow in your mouth
for the spine in your howl
mind & heart & soul - oh the worlds you change
just by blinking in them.

this is it, you are doing it already and yes, in the right way.
now open, a little wider, a little bluer
become a grand space for a grander love.
you will lose things in it, and people too
and everything you feared to admit
was never yours to begin with.

this is the consequence of becoming sky.
flight moves inside us. forests grow and landscapes widen and
it all aches to be held
as we become shelter for whatever comes. for hope. for love.
for each other.
oh the things we find in the opening
between soul & bone.

and the truth is, perhaps
that the world is not here for me
but i here for it
and that changes everything.

TRUST IN THE MYSTERY

to hold the sun and trust in the mystery
and reach center in all things, most often my own —
how

from a seed to know the whole garden
how
and dance for a rain incoming
how
when my doubt is still here
and i give it shelter, tell it stories, sing as if song is the master
and i am the rain incoming

how
to be empowered enough to be powerless, in samadhi
unrelenting surrender, to go amidst the green of the world
and trust my weight to a song with invisible hands

my heart has a thousand eyes and none of them mine
holding visions of a center within and between us

how
am i the self that claims to be me
the me that is you
the us that is god
the god that is both
the seeker and sought
the oneness of all, how, all this
when in sorrow or bliss
i can't seem to fit the stones
on the road back home

i am walking with no feet
circling the infinite arrival

to the pathless mystery

can words arrive at the wordless

not a question but an answer, how,
when the day gifts you tears,
how you string them along your doors like glow lights
and when dullness enters your very soul
how you offer it tea and a blanket
and the night is dark and clear and how, spontaneously, you
sparkle
even when nobody's looking
how you do one thing..

everything you're learning to unlearn
remembering to rejoice at the realignment
rebuilding the reflections resplendent, yes

how you, like this,
are so
so much a something i can't name can't paint can't taste
i can only water

darling whatever doesn't bring you alive
is too small for you
but seeking more of it
makes you smaller

there is no path to enlightenment
you need no keys to the gateless
take your wholeness, like this

and leap